This Notebook Belongs To

___

CPSIA information can be obtained
at www.ICGtesting.com
Printed in the USA
LVHW061232220323
742255LV00007B/178

9 783724 789529